POPULAR SONGS

HAL LEONARD STUDENT PIANO LIBRARY

INTERMEDIATE/LATE INTERMEDIATE PIANO SOLOS

Classic Joplin Rags

Arranged by Fred Kern

D0613754

CONTENTS

ISBN 978-1-4234-4395-7

HAL•LEONARD®

7777 W. BLUEMOUND RD. P.O. BOX 13819 MILWAUKEE, WI 53213

In Australia Contact:
Hal Leonard Australia Pty. Ltd.
4 Lentara Court
Cheltenham, Victoria, 3192 Australia
Email: ausadmin@halleonard.com.au

Visit Hal Leonard Online at
www.halleonard.com

Bethena
(Concert Waltz)

By Scott Joplin
Arranged by Fred Kern

Waltz tempo (♩ = 108)

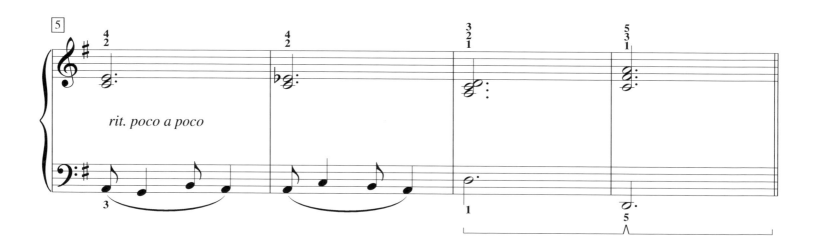

Valse cantabile

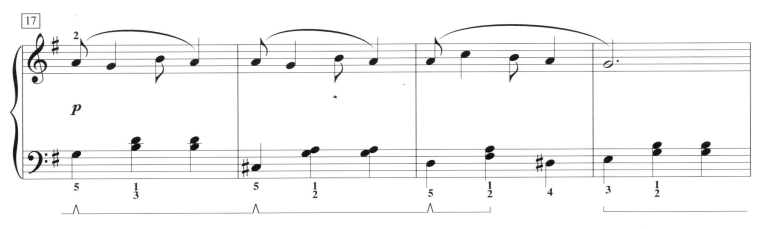

To Coda ⊕

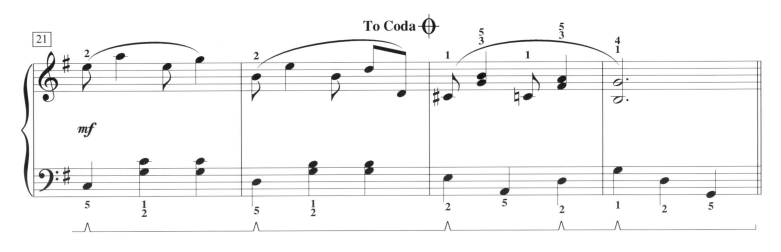

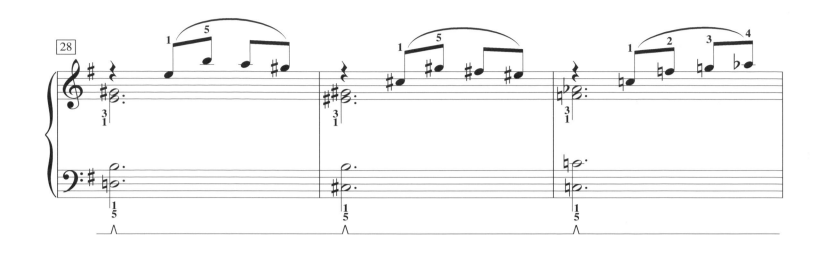

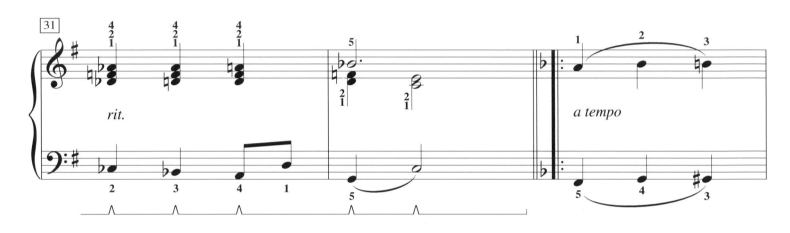

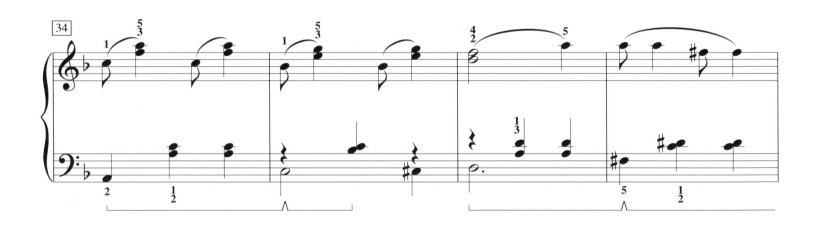

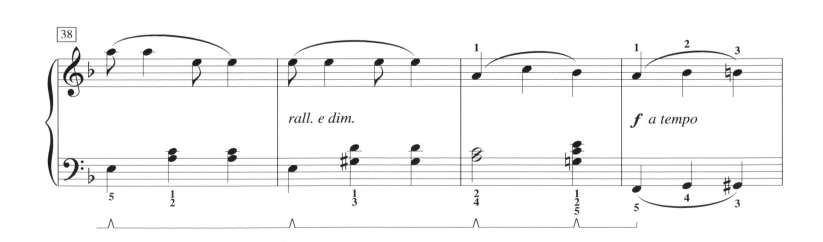

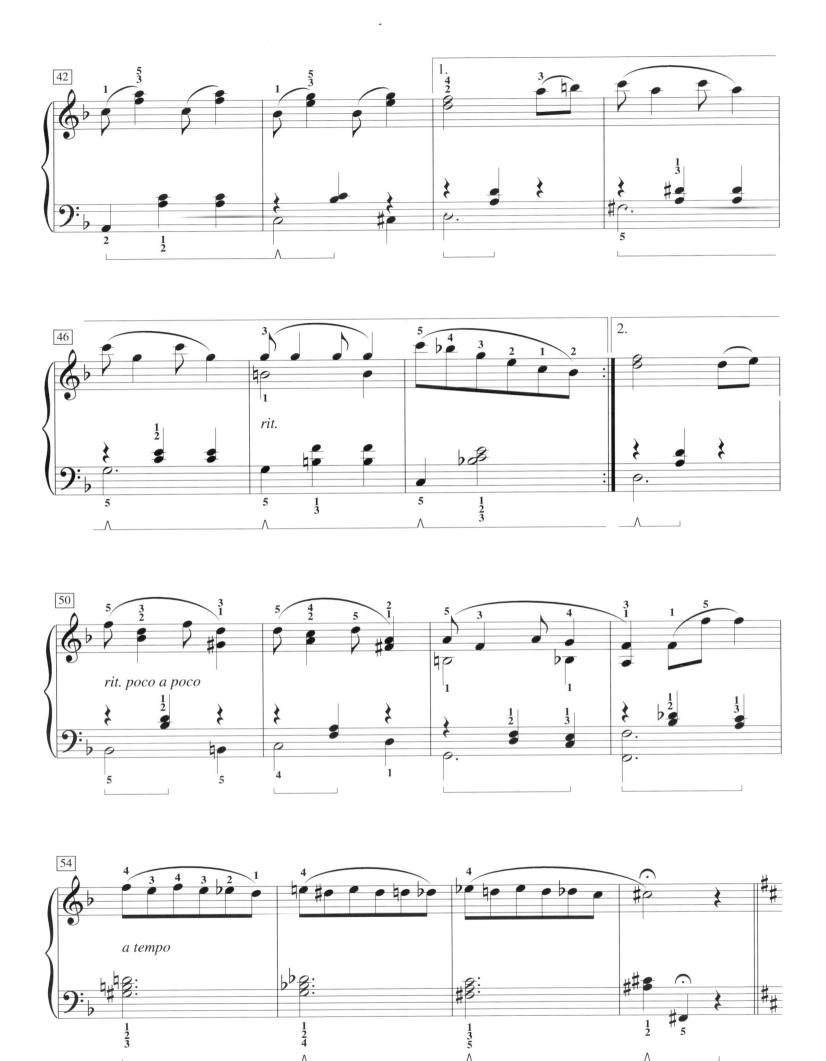

The Entertainer

By Scott Joplin
Arranged by Fred Kern

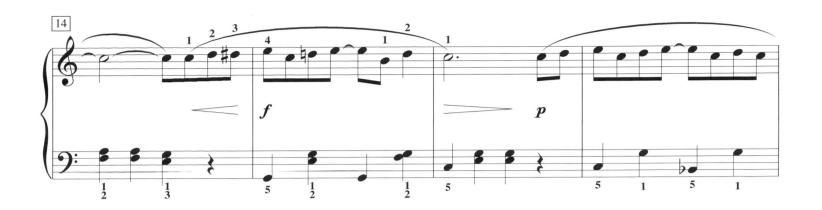

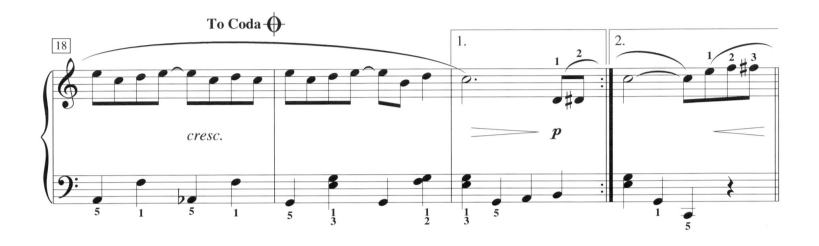

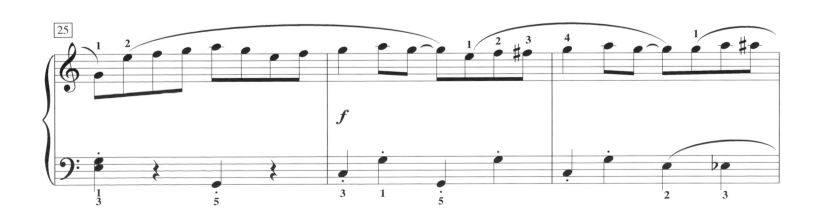

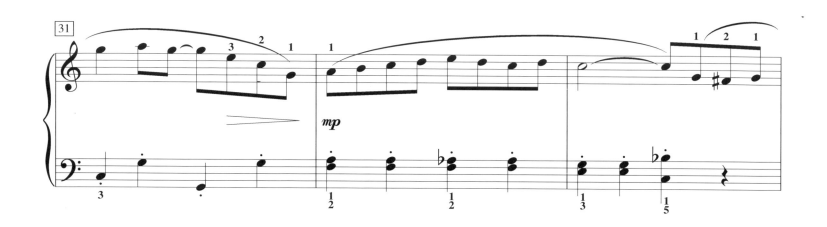

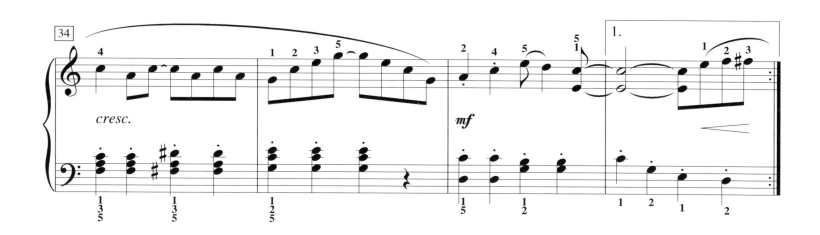

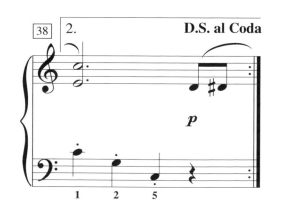

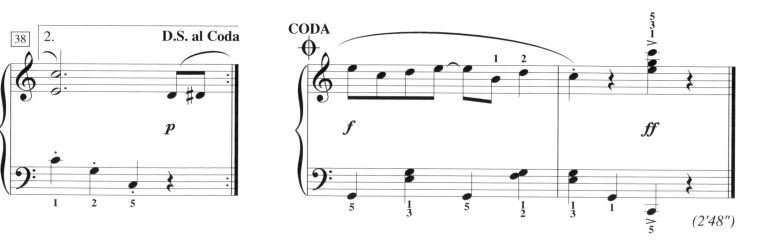

(2'48")

Maple Leaf Rag

By Scott Joplin
Arranged by Fred Kern

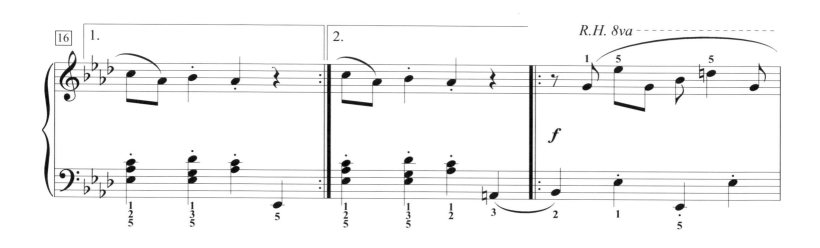

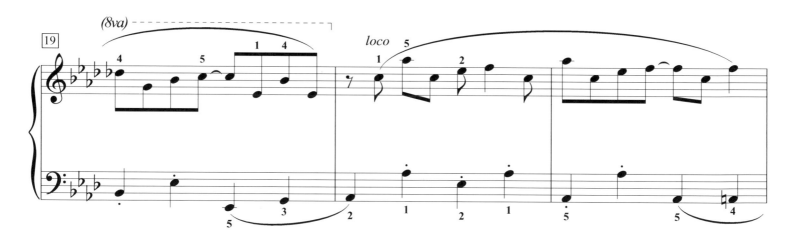

Pineapple Rag

By Scott Joplin
Arranged by Fred Kern

To Coda ⊕

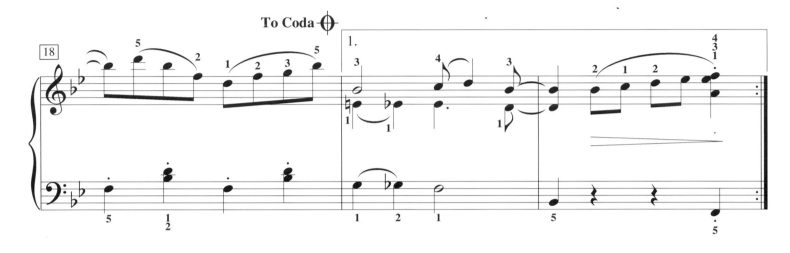

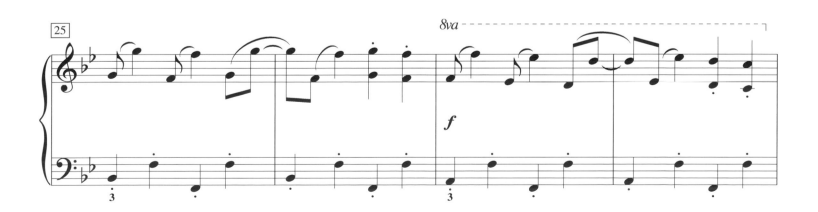

15

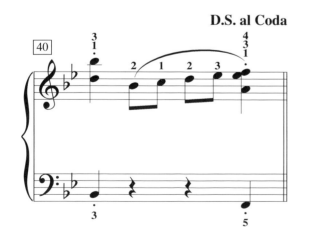

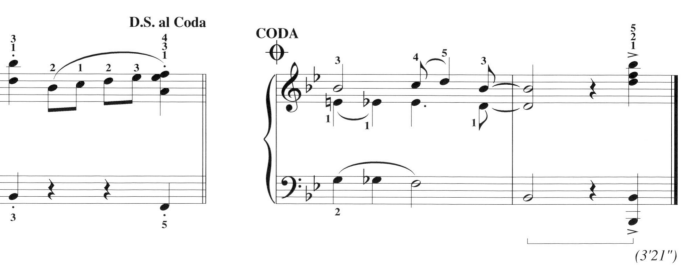

Swipesy

(Cake Walk)

By Scott Joplin and Arthur Marshall
Arranged by Fred Kern

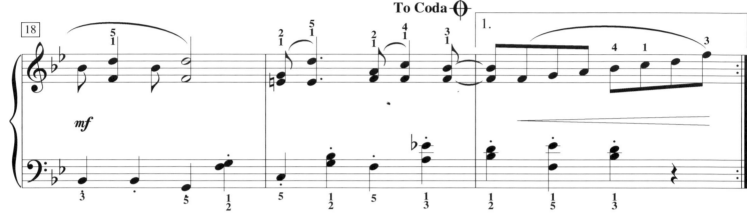

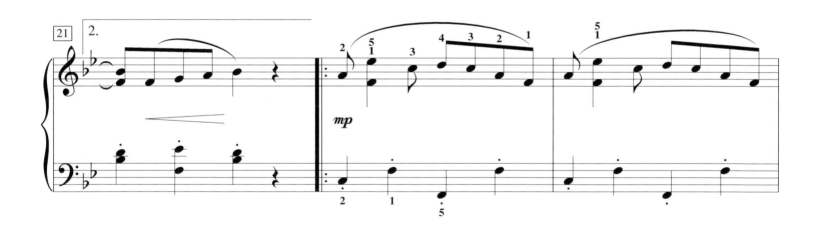

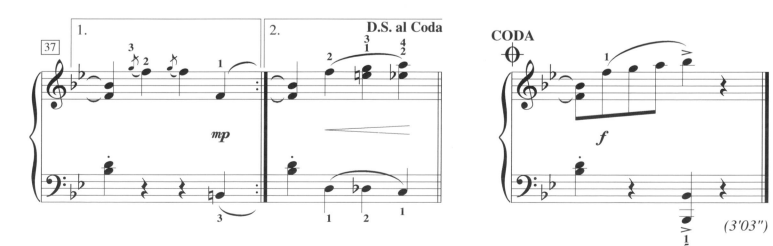

Pleasant Moments

(Ragtime Waltz)

By Scott Joplin
Arranged by Fred Kern

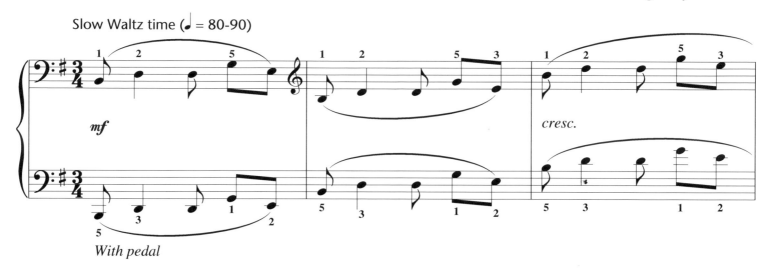

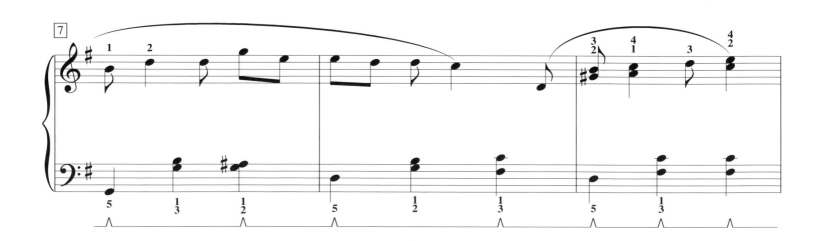